Published by Createspace Publishing, Createspace.com

Project Management Websites

www.PMWebsites.org

Thomas and Thomas, LLP

PO Box 22432

Tampa, FL 33622

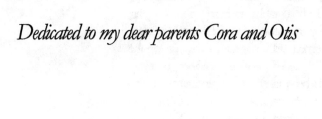

Dedicated to my dear parents Cora and Otis

Table of Contents

About the Author

James Thomas is an experienced project management professional whom has been called on to manage projects for several of the world's largest companies including General Motors, General Dynamics Land Systems, Delphi Automotive, Dow Chemical, EDS, Computer Sciences Corporation, Comsys, U.S. Environmental Protection Agency, Department of Veterans Affairs, State of Michigan, Raytheon, ProQuest.Com, CHEP, and PricewaterhouseCoopers. He was trained by several Orange County, CA project scholars including Paul Konkel and Quentin Fleming who wrote the book <u>Earned Value in Project Management</u>. James Thomas holds a University of Michigan degree and a Certificate in Project Management from the University of California-Irvine. He is also a software developer and has several professional certifications including a PMP certification from PMI, a Cisco CCNA and Network + and A + certifications from Comptia. In addition to managing projects, James is an adjunct-instructor with Remington College and teaches Project Management, Java, Networking and IT Infrastructure. He has managed project communications with websites for many years and decided to share his much sought after skill in this book.

Icon Key

ICON KEY

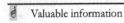 Valuable information

 Web Download

Warning Message

A set of helpful icons have been included to help you

Introduction

We have often noticed that superstar athletes are usually groomed by good coaches. One of my favorite hobbies is coaching. Whether its basketball, computer engineering, start-up businesses or project management communications. To me, there is no thrill greater than helping someone to become highly successful. If you are looking to become a high performer in project management (PM), need a little job security, or just want to sharpen your skills, this book will be a very valuable asset. For many years, I have been able to exceed expectations by using project websites as a communications tool. Many of my clients hire project managers or business analysts to solely handle communications on large projects. It gives the appearance of a well managed project and builds credibility.

Traditionally, when people think of websites they think of them being exposed to the public. As I first began building corporate PM Websites, one of my initial tasks was to explain to clients that we can control whether the site is publicly accessible or only accessible within the company. Knowledge has evolved with the advent of e-Business. We will explore this more later.

Years ago, I started building websites as a hobby. I was working as an engineering program manager for the State of Michigan, but wanted to maintain my skill as a computer geek so I built websites.

As the Internet bubble started to expand, I started receiving calls for openings. I received several offers that I could not refuse and moved into IT full time as a project manager. At first it seemed like a demotion, but the pay was nearly double. It also allowed me to join the modern era, whereas I felt somewhat stagnated in the government bureaucracy. My first corporate project was to build a global e-commerce website for General Dynamics Land Systems. This helped me to learn more about corporate websites, while I earned my Project Management Professional Certification. As I earned my PMP, I really began to see how critical communications were and I saw the value websites could bring. Soon after, I was called on by Delphi Automotive to turn a project around and that's where I built my first project communications website. They were extremely excited and I received a large unexpected project bonus. My success was largely attributed to the PM Website. Now that much of the corporate world has gone global, PM Websites have become even more invaluable in managing project communications. In this book I will take you step by step through the process and provide the tools to build PM Websites and most any type of website for that matter. It won't be nearly as hard as you think and you will find many areas to apply your new skills.

Chapter

1

The Project

Management

Body of

Knowledge

This chapter describes the basics of project
management, which is supported by project websites.

The Project Management Institute (PMI) Body of Knowledge (PMBOK) identifies ten major knowledge areas for project management. This list includes Risk, Scope, Time, Cost, Procurement, Human Resources, Quality, Professional Ethics, Integration, and communications.

Whether you are a formal project manager or what we in the industry call an accidental project manager (wearing a PM hat) you should become familiar with the knowledge areas and their outputs. In project management, one of the biggest challenges is pulling all this information together and making it available to the project stakeholders and team of builders. That's where a project website is invaluable. The following is a review of the knowledge areas as the deliverables of each knowledge are is a likely content candidate for a professional project website. If you are already a project guru you may want to skip to chapter two.

Communication Management

Project managers spend 90% of their time managing communications. Communications management is where the project stakeholders are identified and their communication needs defined. Often project managers or business analysts are hired as dedicated resources for communications only. One of the major outputs of communications management is the Project Website. The project website is where all of the outputs above are stored for the various audiences of a project. Timely communications are invaluable in keeping projects healthy and on-track. The other outputs are Communication Plans, Contact Lists, status reports, forecasts, and meeting minutes.

Risk Management

Risk is one of the most important areas of project management. To be a great project manager is to be a great risk manager. Risk management starts with a simple question. What all can go wrong? The outputs of Risk Management include a risk log and assessments for each risk. The risk should be stated in an IF, THEN format. For example:

1) **If** the backup tape does not restore properly, **then** the code will have to be rebuilt.

2) **If** the temperature rises above 98 degrees, **then** the bonding cement will dry too quickly and will have to be redone.

3) **If** a key resource is lost, **then** the defects will take twice as long to fix.

Issues - Issues are questions that, if unanswered, will prevent the project from completing successfully.

Issue Management is not a formal knowledge area, however it is critical that issues be tracked and resolved as quickly as possible. An issue log is an essential document used to track issues.

Scope Management

The scope of the project identifies all of the work tasks that have to be completed.

The outputs are Work Breakdown Structure (WBS), Scope Statement, requirements summary, Specifications, Use Cases, Business Rules, Assumptions and Constraints, etc. A Project Charter or Vision Document will typically be completed prior to the project being implemented, but may be developed in this process as well. As projects progress, change requests and change control documents arise from this process.

Time Management

Time management includes the scheduling and sequencing of the tasks. Basically, this is where we determine the project duration. The outputs are the project schedule, the critical path task list, pert charts, dependencies, and iteration plans.

Cost Management

Cost management identifies the cost of each task and associated equipment to determine the budget, which is often constrained. The outputs are the Project Budget and Earned Value parameters and measurements.

Quality Management

Quality management identifies the level of quality the product or services is required to adhere to. We are often constrained between cost, time or quality, which is a cause for project stress. If you want it now then it won't be perfect. If you want it cheaper then it may not be quick or perfect. If you want it perfect then you will have to pay more and it will likely take longer.

There are also many global, national, local, or organizational standards that the product or service must meet. Also, there may be specifications or guidelines that must be followed in the development of the product or service. These are identified in the Quality Management process. As the product or service is being developed statistical control charts and inspection charts may be generated as part of this process.

Human Resources Management

Most projects require human resources, which can be contract, permanent or sometimes often a combination of the two. The outputs can be position descriptions, resumes, offer letters, hiring criteria, citizenship and visa guidelines, performance objectives, time sheets, etc.

Procurement Management

Procurement management entails the acquisition of resources to complete the project. The outputs may include contracts, sub-contracts, bid solicitations, bid submittals, request for quotes, proposals, etc.

Professional Ethics

Professional Ethics are rules that guide actions in business. It is just common sense. We have to uphold the highest standards of human character due to our role as leaders. The outputs may include corporate policies, acceptance agreements, etc. Since the Enron debacle, the Sarbanes-Oxley act has forced many companies to take professional ethics seriously. Project managers are responsible for maintaining compliance with these regulations as well as every leader in the corporation.

Integration Management

Integration management is a very special knowledge area. In my experience as a project manager it is where most issues are discovered. Therefore, a good integration plan is mandatory. It is where all of the products, processes, teams, and distribution networks come together. Most projects are composed of different components, modules, iterations, and design tracks being built by different individuals. Often in system development, batch jobs, web services or messaging services are used for transmission of data. This is often the source of integration issues or defects. This requires is a considerable effort to bring the disparate parts together. Even the smoothest projects have integration issues. The outputs of Integration Management are Integration Plans, Integration Specifications, and Integration Agreements.

Chapter

2

HTML Basics

In this chapter you will learn the basics of HTML which all websites are based on.

You will need MS Internet Explorer and MS Notepad, both are included with your MS Windows desktop .

H TML is not a programming language like Visual Basic or Java. It stands for Hyper Text Markup Language. Therefore, it deals more with the display of text on the screen. Similar to the way we format words in a document as bold, underline, and colored. If you are already an HTML expert, you may want to skip the rest of this chapter.

HTML provides a way of taking mundane machine-like text on a server, such as a file directory and allows it to be presented in a more meaningful and useful way. HTML is very easy to use; it was designed that way. You don't have to be a programmer to use it. If you can edit a text file, or a MS Word document then you can write HTML (and if you can write email, you can edit a text file). If you tried to learn before and couldn't, then just come in with an open mind and let me coach you.

In this chapter, you'll create small pages and view them. There aren't really any "required" exercises, but you should play with the concepts until you're comfortable with them.

When creating file names, a good naming convention is to capitalize each word and avoid using spaces for readability and standardization, for example: **BackPageView or MainProgram.** The file name should always represent what the file does or what it contains.

First "Hello World" Web Page

We will first develop HTML using Notepad and then move to MS FrontPage in the next chapter. These first pages are only visible on your workstation. We will cover publishing the web pages for others to see in a later chapter. To create your first sample web page, follow these steps.

1.   Using a Windows desktop, launch Notepad by selecting (Windows **Start | Programs | Accessories | Notepad**).

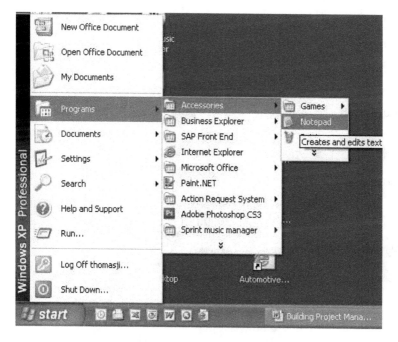

Figure 1

2.   Give the file a name by saving it to your desktop as Hello.htm. (Always give your HTML files names ending in

(".html" or ".htm")). In Notepad select **File | Save As | Desktop |** enter Hello.htm. Set the **Save as Type | All Files.**

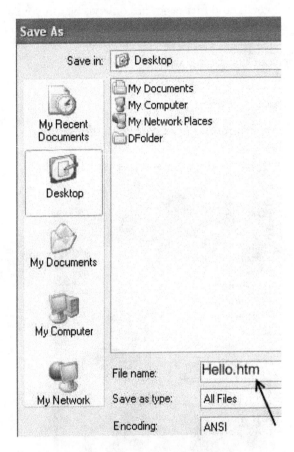

Figure 2

3.   Type "Hello World!" and save the file. Select **File | Save**.

Figure 3

4. From your windows desktop, launch your Internet Explorer browser. Select **Start | Programs | Internet Explorer**

5. Open your first sample web page. Select **File | Open | Browse | Desktop** and then select **Hello.htm**. The file will likely have a blue Explorer icon in front of it.

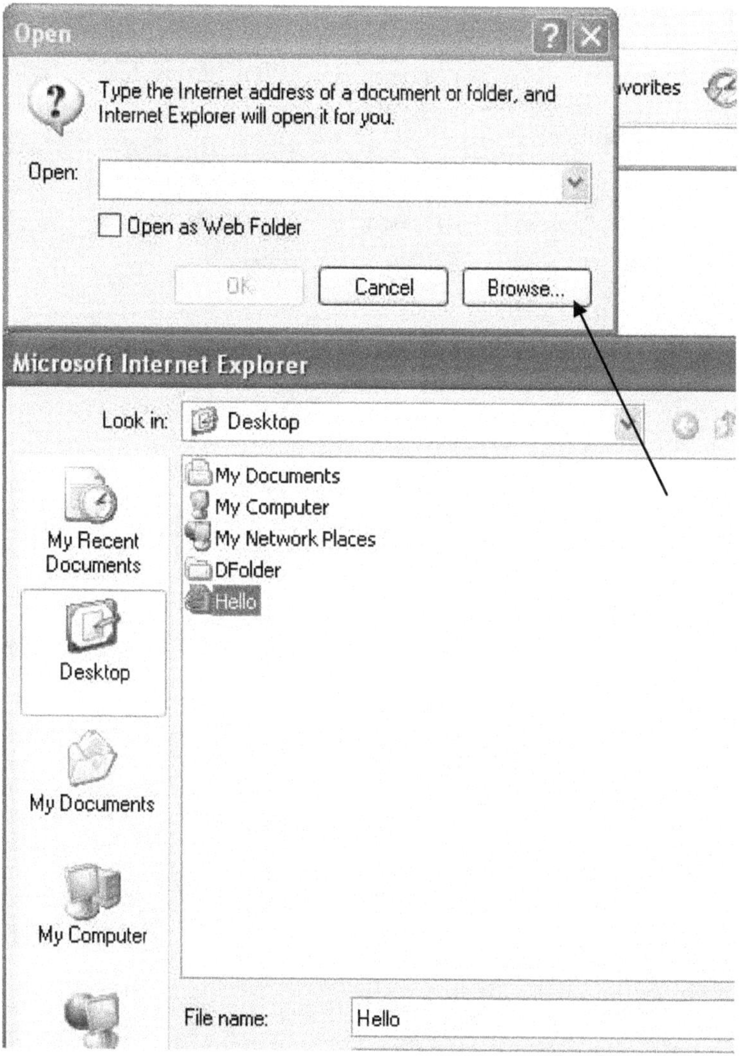

Open ? ×

Type the Internet address of a document or folder, and
Internet Explorer will open it for you.

Open: [   ] ▾

☐ Open as Web Folder

OK   Cancel   Browse...

Microsoft Internet Explorer

Look in: 📁 Desktop ▾ ◷ 🔍

My Documents
My Computer
My Network Places
DFolder
Hello

My Recent
Documents

Desktop

My Documents

My Computer

File name: Hello

Figure 4

6.   This will display your first Hello World web page in your browser. It may not be very impressive, but we have to start with the basics.

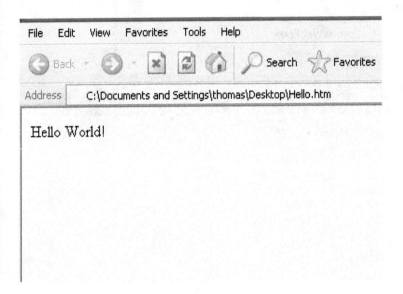

Figure 5

Now that you have created your first page, here are some more options to try.

Go back to Notepad and open the Hello.htm file again. This time type <b>Hello World!</b>. You will see that the tag <b> marks the text as bold and the </b> tag cancels the bold markup. Save it using **File | Save**.

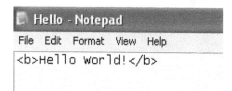

Figure 6

In your browser, use the "Refresh" function to view each change after saving in Notepad.

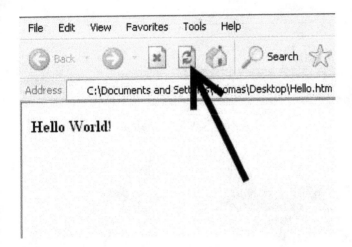

Figure 7

Next go back to Notepad and type the following:

<html>

<head>

<title>Hello World!</title>

</head>

<body>

Hello World!

</body>

</html>

```
Untitled - Notepad
File  Edit  Format  View  Help
<head>
<title>Hello world!</title>
</head>
<body>
Hello world!
</body>
</html>
```

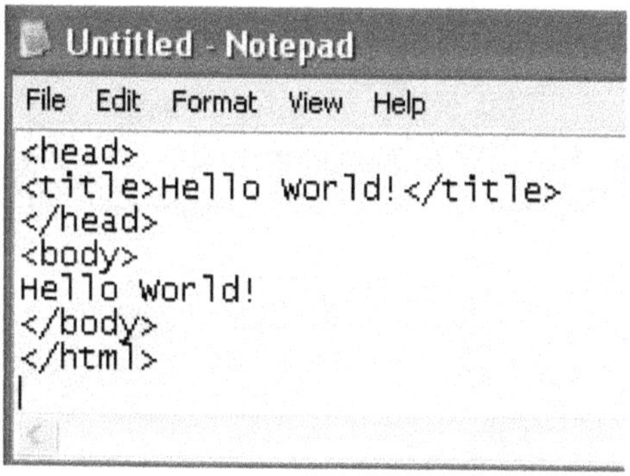

Figure 8

Remember to save in Notepad using **File | Save.** In your browser, use the "Refresh" function to view the change.

☞ If you can't see the change in the browser it is likely because you have not saved the text in Notepad.

Figure 9

The <title> tag changes the blue title bar at the very top of the browser window. If you don't want a title, leave out the lines beginning with <head>, <title>, and </head>.

Try these headings:

<h1>Hello World!</h1>

<h2> Hello World!</</h2>

Figure 10

If you don't want a title, leave out the lines beginning with <head>, <title>, and </head>. Each paragraph you write should start with a <p> tag. The </p> is optional, unlike the end tags for elements like headings. For example:

<p>This is the first paragraph.</p>

<p>This is the second paragraph.</p>

To add a bit of emphasis, you can emphasize one or more words with the <em> tag, for instance:

This is a really <em>interesting</em> topic!

Adding Pictures

Pictures make your pages come alive and provide much more information than words. To add an image we use the <img> tag. Find a picture on your computer and save it to the desktop as **TestPic.jpg**. (If you don't have one handy you can use the My Computer folder and navigate to **C:\windows\system32\oobe\images**. Select an image with a .jpg extension and save it to the desktop as TestPic.jpg.)

As you search for a picture, if you move the mouse cursor over a picture filename it will display a box with the dimensions of the file. Let's assume the picture is 200 pixels wide by 150 pixels high. Type the following line in your file in Notepad:

<img src="TestPic.jpg" width="200" height="150">

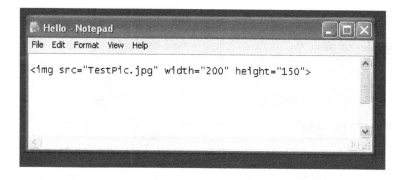

Figure 11

Save the file as Hello2.htm.

✐ It is important that the picture be in the same file location as the web page otherwise it will not render. You may get a frame with a red X.

Figure 12

You will either need to copy the image into the folder where the web page resides or place the name of folder where the image resides in front of the file name with a "/" such as **<img border="0" src="images/smallpic.jpg" width="35" height="22">** The src attribute names the image file. The width and height aren't strictly necessary but help to speed the display of your Web page. There is one more step for people who can't see the image or have image display turned off to speed up their browsing. In the absence of physical image you will need a description that they can read instead. You can add a short description as follows:

<img src="TestPic.jpg" width="200" height="150" alt="My Test Image">

The **alt** attribute is used to give the short description, in this case "My Test Image".

Open the file in your browser to view the picture.

Adding line breaks

If you would like to move text to a separate line, use the <br> tag. For example:

This is a test

This is another test.

Adding links to other pages

What makes the Web so effective is the ability to define links from one page to another, and to follow links at the click of a button. A single click can take you to another server in another country!

Links are defined with the <a> tag. Let's create a link to the page defined in the file "Hello2.htm". Make sure they are both on the desktop or in the same folder as the HTML file you are editing: Open Hello.htm in Notepad. Type the following tag and save it:

<a href="hello2.htm"> My Hello page</a>.

Open the Hello.htm in your browser to view the link.

The text between the <a> and the </a> is used as the caption for the link. It is common for the caption to be in blue underlined text.

Adding lists

The easiest type of list is a bulleted list, often called an unordered list. It uses the <ul> and <li> tags, for instance:

```
<ul>

<ul>

<li> item 1</li>

<li> item 2 </li>

<li> item 3 </li>

</ul>
```

Email Links

Email also uses the <a tag. For an email link, as defined below set **href** to "mailto:email-address". For example:

<a href="mailto:webmaster@pmwebsites.org">the Webmaster </a>

This will launch an email to the Webmaster at the pmwebsites.org using your default email system.

```
Hello - Notepad
File  Edit  Format  View  Help
<a href="hello2.htm"> My Hello page</a>


<ul>
<ul>
  <li> item 1</li>
  <li> item 2 </li>
  <li> item 3 </li>
</ul>
|
<a href="mailto:webmaster@pmwebsite.org">the Webmaster</a>
```

Figure 13

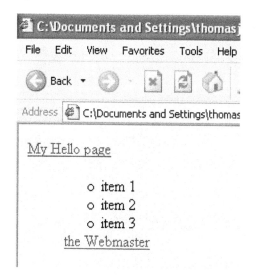

Figure 14

Comments

You can put comments in your HTML file that won't display on the Web page. This lets you explain why your HTML code is a certain way, to anyone viewing your HTML source code. This may be someone else, or (more likely) it may be you at some point in the future.

Start a comment with "<!--" and end it with "-->", like

<!-- This is a comment, and won't display to the user -->

<!-- comment examples inserted by JSM on 9-23-96, for clarity -->

This provides a basic overview of HTML. Many websites are built with pure HTML, but in the next chapter we will explore a tool that simplifies the building of HTML. Please see the reference section for more tutorials and information on raw HTML if you are interested.

Chapter

3

MS Front Page

Basics

In this chapter you will learn the basics of MS FrontPage, a tool that greatly simplifies the building of websites.

HTML is generated automatically by MS FrontPage by dragging and dropping objects such as pictures, tables, and web controls onto the open page. You will also find the common formatting tool bars and menus that are found in MS Word and other MS products for the screen.

FrontPage Screen Layout

Below is a diagram of the default page layout in FrontPage. You can change the tool bars at the top by selecting **View | Tool Bars.** You can also change the page view by selecting a different **View** option at the bottom of the right panel.

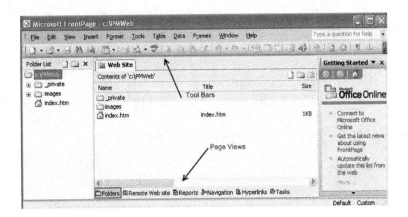

Figure 15

Views

Page view gives you a WYSIWYG editing environment for creating and editing web pages.

Folders view lists all of the files and folders in your web for easy management.

Reports view identifies problems with pages and links in the web including slow-loading pages, broken links, and other errors.

Navigation view lists the navigation order of the site and allows you to change the order that a user would view the pages.

Hyperlinks view allows you to organize the links in the web pages.

Tasks view provides a grid for inputting tasks you need to complete in your web.

Creating a Web Using the Web Wizard

Open FrontPage and select **File|New|Web...** from the menu bar or click the small down arrow next to the **New** button on the standard toolbar and select **Web....**

Figure 16

Select the type of web you want to create. It is usually best to create a simple **One Page Web** which you can add additional blank pages to as you need them. Enter a location on your computer for the new web in the edit box provided. Append the name TestWeb to the end of text. Such as **C:\Documents and Setting\User\My Documents\My Webs\TestWeb**. This is the location where you can preview the web on your computer. Later, the website will need to be copied to the server to be viewed by other users on your intranet or on the internet.

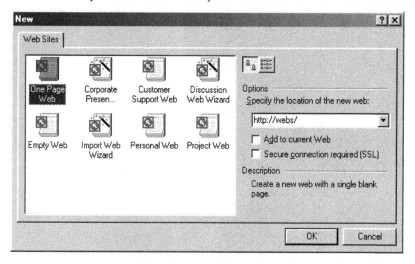

Figure 17

Click **OK** and wait for FrontPage to finish creating the web.

Now, explore your web. Click **Folders view** to see the initial page (default.htm) that was created and two folders. The "images" folder is where you will place all your graphics and photos. While it is not imperative that the images be placed in a separate folder, it keeps the web organized.

Click on **Reports view | Site Summary** to see a list of reports for the site. As you construct your web, this page will be much more useful. From here, you can identify and correct broken hyperlinks and fix large pages that take a long time to load.

View the navigation layout of the web by clicking **Navigation view**. Right now, there is only one page - the home page - listed. As more pages are added, this page becomes helpful to see how all your pages are linked together.

The Hyperlinks view allows you to manage the links on your pages.

Optional - in Tasks view, list the tasks that need to be accomplished to create the web. Select **Edit | Task | Add Tasks** to add a task. Or click the down arrow beside the New button on the standard toolbar.

Make pages and save them, marking them as completed in the task view.

Click **Folders** view to locate the next page to work on.

Adding a Web Page from a Template

FrontPage provides a few simple page templates that can be added to a web. Follow these steps to add a template to a web page.

Select **File | New | Page...** and if you want a blank page select Normal Page or choose a template such as the Feedback Form.

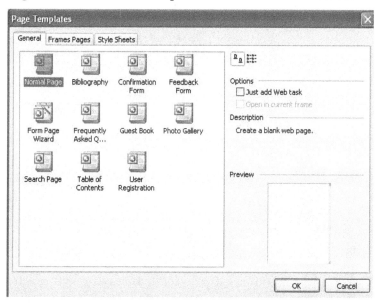

Figure 18

Select a template and click **OK**.

Replace the place-holding body text with your own text and photos with images you would like on your web page. Remember to save your work afterwards.

Report View

When your web is completed, click **Reports** view to verify that links are correct and use the **Reporting** toolbar to switch between reports. The primary elements to check for are "Broken Links", which are links that do not yield a page or file.

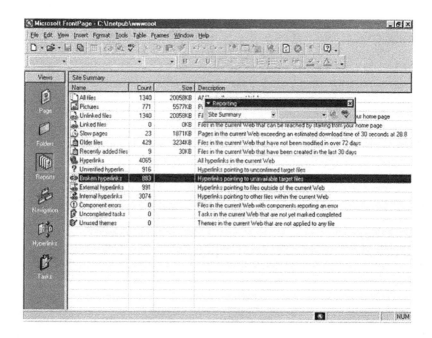

Figure 19

Open A Web

To open a web you have already created, select **File | Open Web...** from the menu bar. Select the web folder from the list and click **Open**.

Design View

When you first open an .htm or .html file the default is the Design View. In this view you can drag and drop objects such has pictures and forms.

Code or HTML View

There will eventually be times when you have to go into the code because some element on the page will not render properly or you just need to get finer detail into the page. You can select the **Code** or **HTML** tab at the bottom of the design window. (depending on the version of MS Frontpage that you are using.

Split View

For Frontpage 2003 users. The Split view gives you the best of both worlds. You can see the design and the code at the same time. Select the **Split** at the bottom of the Design window.

Preview View

Preview applies the formatting and renders a view that is similar to how the page will look in a web browser. Select the **Preview** tab at the bottom of the Design window.

Preview in Internet Explorer

To really see how the page will look, you will have to open it in Internet Explorer. First, you will need to save your work and then select the **Preview in Internet Explorer** icon. It also provides a drop-down list that allows you to render your page in different screen resolutions. Seldom do all users have the same resolution.

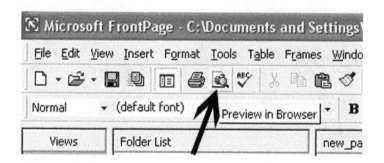

Figure 20

Building Basic Project

Management Documents

In this chapter you will begin to build your Project Management documents referenced in Chapter 1 and convert them to HTML for display on your web.

DOWNLOAD FILES FROM

WWW.PMWEBSITES.ORG

F irst you will need to download the web templates from the www.PMWebsites.org site. Store the files into the **My Documents|My Webs** folder. As you customize each document, it must be stored in the **My Documents|My Webs|PMWeb|Docs** folder. Some of the templates are IT related, but can be customized for any industry.

Feel free to skip any templates that do not apply. Also, for most project documents, we will create an HTML version, but maintain the native file format for editing with MS Word, Excel, etc.

Communications Plan

The communications plan is critical in identifying who gets what information and in what format and frequency.

Open the **My Documents|My Webs|PMWeb|Docs** folder. Then, open the **CommunicationsPlan** template in MS Word. Add the information that is pertinent to your project into the template. After adding your information, save the template as a document with a .doc extension. **File|Save As** [Save as Type: Word Document] Next, create an HTML version of the document by using **File| Save as Web Page.** But, don't save it in the Docs folder. Save it in the **My Documents|My Webs|PMWeb** folder under the name CommunicationsPlan.htm. To verify that the filename was saved correctly, select it from the Folder List, right-click on its file name. Then view the properties. If the Folder List is not open, Select **View | Folder List**.

Risk Plan

The risk plan helps us to identify what can go wrong so that we can mitigate it.

Open the **My Documents|My Webs|PMWeb|Docs** folder. Then, open the **RiskPlan** template in MS Word. Add the risks that are pertinent to your project into the template. After adding your risks, save the template as a document with a **.doc** extension. **File|Save As** [Save as Type: Word Document]. Next, create an HTML version of the document by using **File| Save as Web Page.** But, don't save it in the Docs folder. Save it in the **My Documents|My Webs|PMWeb** folder under the name **RiskPlan..htm.** To verify that the filename was saved correctly, select it from the Folder List, right-click on its file name. Then view the properties. If the Folder List is not open, Select **View|Folder List**.

Project Charter

The project charter defines the goals of the project and officially establishes the project.

Open the **My Documents|My Webs|PMWeb|Docs** folder. Then, open the **ProjectCharter** template. Add the information that is pertinent to your project into the template. After adding your information, save the template as a document with a **.doc** extension.

File | Save As [Save as Type: Word Document] Next, create an HTML version of the document by using **File | Save as Web Page.** But, don't save it in the Docs folder. Save it in the **My Documents | My Webs | PMWeb** folder.

Issue Log

Issues are questions that, if unanswered, will prevent the project from completing successfully.

Open the **My Documents | My Webs | PMWeb | Docs** folder. Then, open the **IssueLog** template. Add the issues information that is pertinent to your project into the template. After adding your information, save the template as a document with a **.doc** extension. **File | Save As** [Save as Type: Word Document] Next, create an HTML version of the document by using **File | Save as Web Page.** But, don't save it in the Docs folder. Save it in the **My Documents | My Webs | PMWeb** folder.

Project Schedule

You will need to create a project schedule using Microsoft Project. Before you open MS project:

> 1) Have your team of builders define the tasks based on your project scope and WBS using post it notes on a white board

2) Have your team estimate the effort for each task on the notes using best case, most likely and worst case estimates. Break tasks down in 40 hour increments or less. A 40 hour increment allows you to have weekly tasks to report on your weekly status report to leadership.

3) Have your team define the dependencies such as what must be done first, second, etc. Create your precedence chart. By moving the post it notes in the order of what goes first second etc.

4) Define your critical path and duration by adding up the longest path thru the network of post it notes.

5) After defining your duration, see if some of the tasks can be done in parallel to shorten the overall duration.

If you follow these steps, when you open MS Project it will be just a simple matter of data entry. If you don't follow this sequence your schedule could get very unwieldy very fast.

Now that you have defined your project as outlined above, we can begin with MS Project. If your organization does not provide a standard project template, MS Project comes with some. **File|New|Templates|On My Computer.** One last thing before starting your work. Set the Autosave option using **Tools|Options|Save|Autosave.** Enter your Main Title on the first line. Group your sub-tasks under your defined phases or iterations.

Remember to add milestones. Your duration should equal your duration that was defined on the board in post it notes.

After you are satisfied with your schedule, save it as your baseline using **Tools | Tracking | Save Baseline**. By saving your baseline you will be able to track your progress as tasks are completed using **Project | Project Information | Statistics**.

Next, save your project in the **My Documents | My Webs | PMWeb | Docs** folder. Then save it as a Web page using **File | Save as Web Page**. But, don't save web version in the Docs folder. Save it in the **My Documents | My Webs | PMWeb** folder. Save the file name as **PMSchedule and the .htm** filename extension will be added automatically.

Requirements Document

Requirements are defined by the customer(s) and typically detail the specific items that make up the scope of the project.
Depending on the tool preference of the organization, they can be stored in a database or simply a MS Word Document.

Open the **My Documents | My Webs | PMWeb | Docs** folder. Then, open the **Requirements** template. Add the Requirements that are pertinent to your project into the template. After adding your information, save the template as a document with a **.doc** extension.

File | Save As [Save as Type: Word Document] Next, create an HTML version of the document by using **File | Save as Web Page.** But, don't save it in the Docs folder. Save it in the **My Documents | My Webs | PMWeb** folder.

Scope Management Plan

The Scope Management Plan defines the tasks will be performed. It includes the Work Breakdown Structure as well as the change management plan. MS Visio Org Charts can be used to develop the electronic Work Breakdown Structure as well as a great tool called WBSPRO.

Open the **My Documents | My Webs | PMWeb | Docs** folder. Then, open the **ScopeManagementPlan** template. Add the WBS elements that are pertinent to your project into the template. After adding your information, save the template as a document with a **.doc** extension. **File | Save As** [Save as Type: Word Document] Next, create an HTML version of the document by using **File | Save as Web Page.** But, don't save it in the Docs folder. Save it in the **My Documents | My Webs | PMWeb** folder.

Meeting Minutes

Meeting minutes should be collected for each meeting of the project stakeholders. These meetings are typically held weekly as defined in the Communications plan. Typically, a standard Agenda format and Minutes format is used. Depending on the project, these can be detailed "who said what" or just bullets. The main items that should be noted are decisions or action items that arise from the meetings. If the standing agenda is followed, then taking minutes is quite easy.

Open the **My Documents|My Webs|PMWeb|Docs** folder. Then, open the **MeetingMinutes** template. Add the pertinent items from you meetings. After adding your information, save the template as a document with a **.doc** extension. **File|Save As** [Save as Type: Word Document] Next, create an HTML version of the document by using **File| Save as Web Page.** But, don't save it in the Docs folder. Save it in the **My Documents|My Webs|PMWeb** folder.

Quality Plan

The Quality Plan outlines the level of testing and any formal quality thresholds that must be met. If your organization has a quality policy then it should be referenced and integrated into the plan.

Open the **My Documents|My Webs|PMWeb|Docs** folder. Then, open the **QualityPlan** template. Add the Quality Elements that are pertinent to your project into the template. After adding your information, save the template as a document with a **.doc** extension. **File|Save As** [Save as Type: Word Document] Next, create an HTML version of the document by using **File| Save as Web Page.** But, don't save it in the Docs folder. Save it in the **My Documents|My Webs|PMWeb** folder.

Procurement Plan

The procurement plan identifies all resources that must be procured. This includes contractors and equipment. Typically, internal staff is not included. It outlines how resources will be brought onto and taken off of the project.

Open the **My Documents|My Webs|PMWeb|Docs** folder. Then, open the **ProcurementPlan** template. Add the Procurement Items that are pertinent to your project into the template. After adding your information, save the template as a document with a **.doc** extension. **File|Save As** [Save as Type: Word Document] Next, create an HTML version of the document by using **File| Save as Web Page.** But, don't save it in the Docs folder. Save it in the **My Documents|My Webs|PMWeb** folder.

Resource Management Plan

The resource plan identifies how many of what type of resource will be needed. It typically includes the internal and external staff and how many hours are needed.

Open the **My Documents|My Webs|PMWeb|Docs** folder. Then, open the **ResourcePlan** template. Add the Resources that are pertinent to your project into the template. After adding your information, save the template as a document with a **.doc** extension. **File|Save As** [Save as Type: Word Document] Next, create an HTML version of the document by using **File| Save as Web Page.** But, don't save it in the Docs folder. Save it in the **My Documents|My Webs|PMWeb** folder.

Chapter 5

Building Your Custom Project Website

 **PMWEB TEMPLATES NEEDED**

In this chapter you will build your project website from a template using MS FrontPage.

F irst you will need to download the PMWeb templates from www.PMWebsites.Org if you have not already done so. Store the files into the My **Documents|My Webs** folder. Second, will need to store the outputs form each of the previous PM Knowledge areas in the **My Documents|My Webs|PMWeb|Docs** folder.

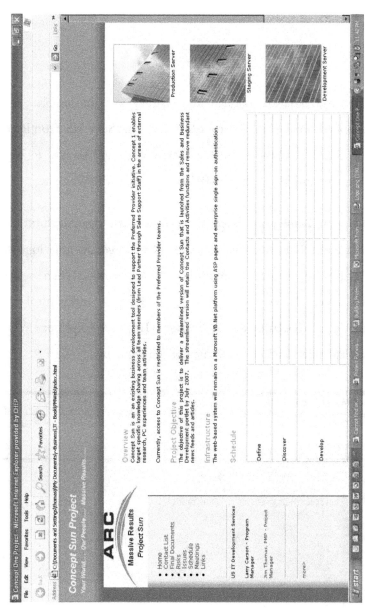

Figure 21

61

Site Construction Tasks

The tasks required to build the website from the template are identified under the MS FrontPage task list. Start MS FrontPage and Select **File|Open Site or Open Web** and browse to **My Documents|My Webs|PMWeb**. Open the **PMWeb site**.

Add your Flash text - Select **View|folder list**. Open **flash.txt** file from the folder list. Place the name of your website after **logo=**. Place your slogan or motto after **&slogan=**. Then select **file|save**. To view your flash logo, Open the **index.html** file then select **file|preview in browser|Internet Explorer**. You can also select Preview from the bottom menu bar.

R E M I N D E R

Remember to go back and select Design or Normal because you can not edit in Preview mode.

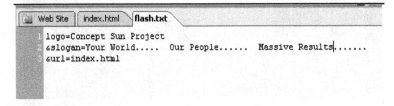

```
    Web Site    index.html    flash.txt
  logo=Concept Sun Project
  &slogan=Your World.....  Our People......  Massive Results.......
  &url=index.html
```

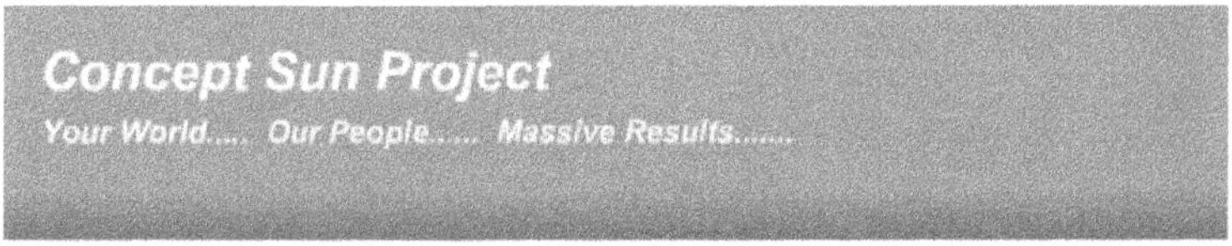

Concept Sun Project
Your World..... Our People..... Massive Results.......

Figure 22

Add your Logo – You will need a picture of your logo saved in .jpg or .gif format. Save or copy your logo into the **My Documents|My Webs|PMWeb|Picts** folder. Open the **index.html** file. If you are following the steps in sequence it will already be open. Just close Internet Explorer and make sure you are in MS FrontPage in Design or Normal mode. Right-click on the picture of the "ARC" logo. Select **Picture Properties|General| Browse,** then select your logo that you stored in the **Picts** folder and select **OK.** Save the **Index.html** file. To view it select **file|preview in browser|Internet Explorer.**

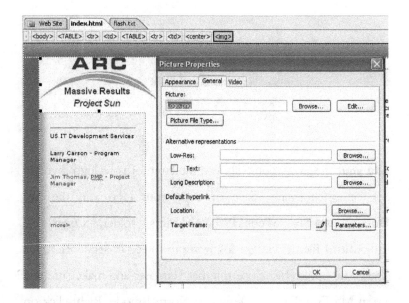

Figure 23

Add your Project Info – Add specific information about your project in the Overview and Project Objectives sections by replacing the text from the template. Copy and paste the title and body text to add additional sections. You don't want to add much more than what the viewer will see when they open the page. You want to avoid them having to scroll if possible to see the main content on the page.

Overview
Concept Sun is an an existing business development tool designed to support the Preferred Provider initiative. Concept 1 enables target specific knowledge sharing across all team members (from Lead Partner through Sales Support Staff) in the areas of external research, PC experiences and team activities.

Currently, access to Concept Sun is restricted to members of the Preferred Provider teams.

Project Objective
The objective of this project is to deliver a streamlined version of Concept Sun that is launched from the Sales and Business Development portlet by July 2007. The streamlined version will retain the Contacts and Activities functions and remove redundant news feeds and articles.

Infrastructure
The web-based system will remain on a Microsoft VB.Net platform using ASP pages and enterprise single sign-on authentication.

Figure 24

Add your Project Schedule – You can add your schedule by simply typing it into the table on index page.

Add a link to your MS Project Schedule – The MS Project Schedule was created in Chapter (4) above and saved as an HTML file in the **PMWeb** folder. There is a file named **menu.js** that references the **PMSchedule** file and launches it from the left menu bar of the **index.htm** home page. Use Notepad to edit the menu.js in older versions of MS Frontpage. To view the schedule Open the **index.html** file then select **file|preview in browser|Internet Explorer.** Then select Schedule from the left menu bar. You can also select Preview from the bottom menu bar.

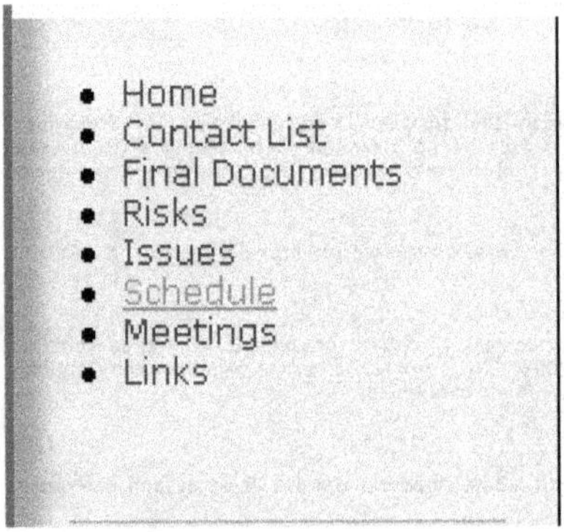

- Home
- Contact List
- Final Documents
- Risks
- Issues
- Schedule
- Meetings
- Links

Figure 25

Add your Server Links – In the software development world there are usually multiple instances of your application running in different environments. Typically, there are Development, Test, Staging and Production server environments. The template uses hyperlinked images to launch each instance. Start Internet Explorer. Browse to your production website. Without closing the browser, bring up MS FrontPage. Open the index..html file. Right-click on the Production Server Image on the right side of the index..html page. Go to **Hyperlink Properties**. Select **Browsed Pages**, then Select the top link in the **Browsed Pages** list, which should be the same link as the page you have open your web browser. Select OK and repeat for other environments that you may have.

Production Server

Staging Server

Development Server

Figure 26

Add a link to your Contact Page – Using Microsoft Word, Open the Communications Plan developed in Chapter 4. Locate the **Project Points of Contact** table. Select the table using Table | Select | Table then do Edit | Copy to copy it. Using MS

FrontPage, open the **ContactList.htm** page. Paste the table using **Edit|PasteSpecial|Normal Paragraph.** Complete any final edits and **Save** the file. To view the Contact List, open the **index.html** file then select **file|preview in browser|Internet Explorer.** Then select Contact List from the left menu bar.

Contact List

Name	Role	Organization	Email	C
John Doe	Program Manager	US IT Development Services	John.Doe@us.com	8
Gary Flowers	Business Analyst	US IT Development Services	Gary.Flowers@us.com	8 C
Jeff Oscar	Software Engineer	US IT Development Services	jeff@us.com	8 C
Sandi Carr	Operations	US IT Operations	Sandi.Carr@us.com	8

Figure 27

Add your Project Leaders – Open the index..html page. Add the names of key project leaders to the left menu bar. Select the first name and Right-click. Add the email hyperlink using **Hyperlink Properties.** Click the **Email** icon then enter the email address and for newer versions of Front Page, add the subject such as the name of the project. Save and repeat previous steps for other project leaders.

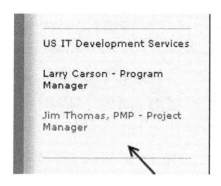

Figure 28

Add your Contact Link – Open the index..html page. Select the **Contact us for more info >** text at the bottom of the page and Right-click. Add the email hyperlink using **Hyperlink|E-mail Address.** Enter the email address of the project manager and name of the project as the subject.

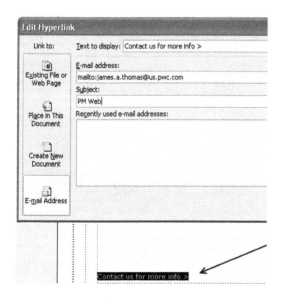

Figure 29

Add links to your Documents – For these steps it is assumed that the project documents are stored in the /docs folder. Open the documents.htm page. Add the title, author and creation date of each project document or work product, typically in alphabetical order. Select the first title and Right-click. Select hyperlink then add the corresponding document from the /docs folder.

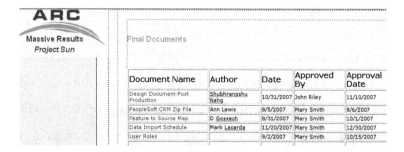

Figure 30

Add your Copy Right Info – The Copyright information will appear in the bottom left corner of every page on the site. Open the **Copyright.js** file. Use Notepad for older versions of MS Front Page. Change the information that is pertinent to your organization. Save the file. . To view the Copyright information, open the **index.html** file then select **file | preview in browser | Internet Explorer.**

Figure 31

Add a link to your Risks – The Risk Plan was created in Chapter 4 and should be accessible from the Risks link located on the primary left navigation bar. If the Risk Plan does not appear, Open the **menu.js** file and verify that the filename in the HREF= is spelled exactly the same as the file name in the Folder List. Its case sensitive. Also, make sure that the **RiskPlan.htm** file is located in the PMWeb folder.

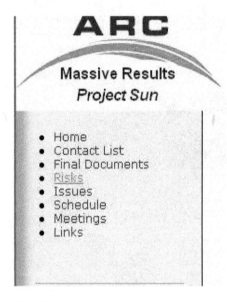

Figure 32

Add your Issues – The IssueLog was created in Chapter 4 and should be accessible from the Issues link located on the primary left navigation bar. If the Issue Log does not appear, Open the **menu.js** file and verify that the filename in the HREF= is spelled exactly the same as the file name in the Folder List. Its case sensitive. Also, make sure that the **IssueLog.htm** file is located in the PMWeb folder. .

Issue Log

Number	Issue	Date	Assigned To

Figure 33

Add your Links – One of the greatest strengths of a website is the convenience of being able to link to other sites. Add every link that your team uses frequently and any that you want to make your users aware of. Open the Links.htm file in MS FrontPage. Add a few words to describe your link. Open your web browser in a separate window. Browse to the target site that you want to add a link for. In MS FrontPage, Right-click on your link description. Select **Hyperlink** then select the target site from the list Browsed Pages. For older versions of MS Front page, click on the browser icon.

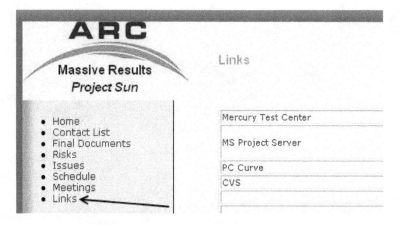

Figure 34

Add your Meetings - For recurring meetings, its important to add the meeting time, days of the week and location information. The conference call numbers and codes should also be included. Open the **MeetingMinutes.htm** file that was created in Chapter 4. Add the pertinent meeting text to the top of the page. Then, add the

Meeting Minutes as links in the table below the meeting information. Add the title, author and creation date of each minutes document, typically in chronological order. Select the first title and Right-click. Select **Hyperlink** then add the corresponding document from folder list. Repeat the steps for each set of Meeting Minutes.

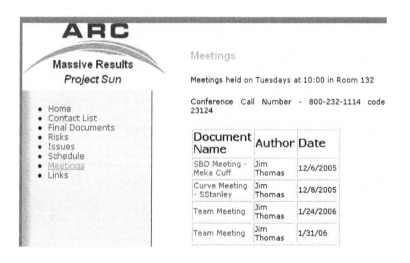

Figure 35

Wireframe Screen Mockups

MS PAINT OR OTHER PHOTO EDITOR NEEDED

In this chapter you will learn how to build wire frame screen mockups used to prototype web applications prior to development.

W ireframes are clickable screen mockups that are developed as prototypes to show what a website *could* look like prior to investing in costly development. They are used to help determine requirements and provide a collaborative platform. Because they respond to user selections, wireframes mimic the actual user interaction with the site. In some cases, they include simple screen captures that are hyperlinked. In other cases, they can include fully developed html with working buttons, tables, data entry controls and forms. In most cases you will need a photo editing tool to store the screens as pictures. You can either use sophisticated software such as Photoshop that may be a bit of overkill for our use here or download a shareware application such as Paint (dot) net from www.Cnet.com under downloads. Paint.net is highly recommended because it allows you to import pictures as layers to overlay on top of other pictures to customize the screens. Otherwise, you can always use the MS Paint, which we will use in our examples as a least common denominator since it's included with MS Windows.

At a high level, to create the wireframe you will need to 1) create a blank website, 2) capture the screens you wish to demo, 3) add the screens to the website as html and 4) link the pages together.

Building a Wireframe - Let's start by creating a website using a standard FrontPage template. Open MS Front page then Select

File|New|One Page Website. You must name the website in the options box so that you will know where to find it. Click on the location edit box and append the word **WireFrame** to the right side of the default location as "**C:\Documents and Settings\thomasj\MyDocuments\MyWebSites\Wireframe**" then, select **OK** to create the site.

W A R N I N G

As you create the new website, you must add the name of the wireframe in the options box so that you will know where to find it later. See figure 34.

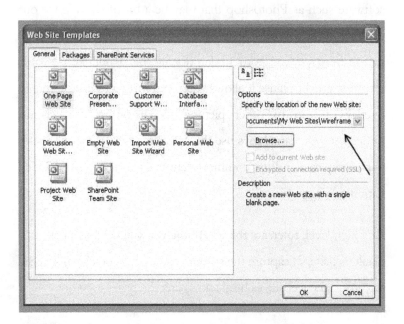

Figure 36

The site files and folders will display in the folder window on the right side of the screen. The index.htm is where you will store your first screen capture of the WireFrame.

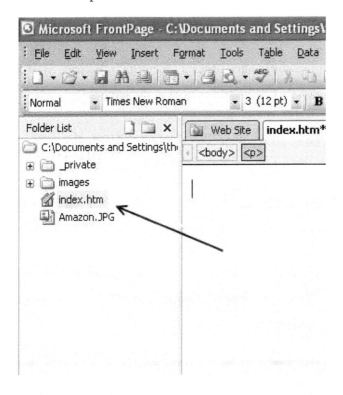

Figure 37

Before we begin, here is an overview of how to Build WireFrames, which consists of the following six steps:

1. Create a blank html page.

   The first time, use the **index.htm** file, which is a blank page. To create additional blank pages **Select**

File | New | Blank Page. Then, **Save | File As** to store it under a name that is representative of the content.

2. Browse to an existing website to use as a starting point

3. Capture the existing page into memory by pressing SHIFT and PRINT SCREEN buttons at the same time

4. Copy the page into a photo editor, such as MS Paint by pressing CTRL - V at the same time

5. Save it as a JPEG picture or PNG for higher resolution in the same folder as the wire frame.

6. Insert the JPEG picture into the blank html page created in Step 1 using **Insert | Picture | From File**. Save it using **File | Save As**.

WARNING

The first page must be saved as **index.htm**. The subsequent pages should be named according to their purpose. The web servers are also case sensitive.

Index.htm will be used as the first page of the WireFrame mockup. Now, let's capture and load the first page. Navigate to a web page such as www.amazon.com. Using your keyboard, while holding down the **Shift Key**, press the **Print Screen** key (usually located at the top towards the right side of your keyboard). Nothing will seem to happen, but this captures the current screen into memory.

Open MS Paint by using **Start | Programs | Accessories | Paint**. A blank canvas will appear. Then, select **Edit | Paste** to load the current screen from memory into Paint. After pasting, the page will appear similar to the following in MS Paint:

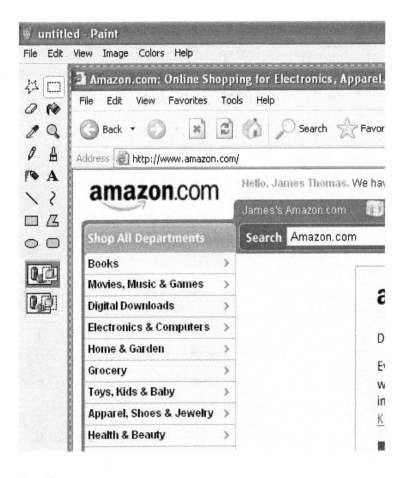

Figure 38

Save the file selecting **File | Save As |** save it to **My Documents/**
My Websites/Wireframe/ Images.

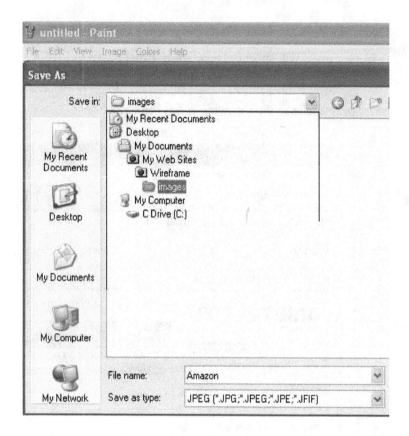

Figure 39

Go back to Front Page to insert the Amazon page picture. Select
the **index.htm** page, which is blank. Select **Insert | Picture | From**
File, then select the **Amazon.jpg** picture and then select **Insert** to
add the picture to the blank canvas. (Alternatively, you can drag
and drop the picture onto the blank html page.) The Amazon

picture should now be displayed in MS Front Page as index.htm.

Remember to **File | Save** to save it.

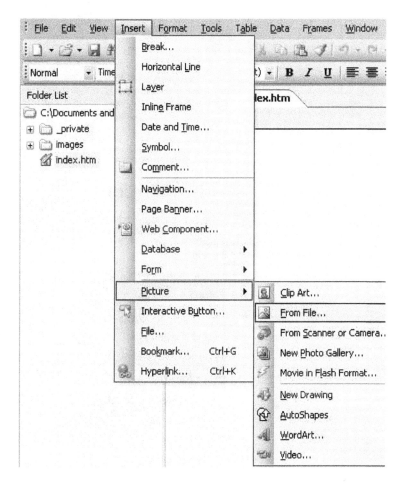

Figure 40

Figure 41

You will repeat the six steps described above to create the next two pages for a three page Wireframe mockup. For this exercise, name the second page Screen2.htm and the third page Screen3.htm. The first page is index.htm.

Linking the index.htm to screen2.htm - Let's start by opening the index.htm file. Select the captured screen picture. Next, you will right-click on the picture to bring up the options menu. Select the **Hyperlink Properties** from the bottom of the menu. This will open the Edit hyperlink window. Select **Screen2.htm** and

OK to complete the link and close the window.

Figure 42

Figure 43

Save the file using File|Save As. The index page is now linked to the Screen2 page.

Linking the screen2.htm to screen3.htm - Open the Screen2.htm file. Select the captured screen picture. Right-click on the picture to bring up the options menu. Select the **Hyperlink**

Properties from the bottom of the menu. This will open the Edit hyperlink window. Select **Screen3.htm** and **OK** to complete the link and close the window. Then, save the index.htm using **File | Save**. The screen2 page is now linked to the screen3 page.

You can test the links by selecting the index.htm and and clicking on the **Preview in Internet Explorer** icon, which launches the web browser. Clicking on the index.htm page will take you to the screen2.htm page and clicking on the screen2.htm page will take you to the screen3.htm page.

WARNING

💣 For the next exercise make sure the Picture Tool bar is visible. Use **View | Tool Bars | Pictures**

Linking from Hotspots - Hotspots can be used to define a smaller region of the page for linking such as a tab, button or text hyperlink. To create a hotspot, use an existing html page that contains a picture. For example, open the index.htm in Front Page. Click on the picture first. Then select the **rectangular hotspot** from the picture tool bar.

Rectangular Hot Spot

Figure 44

Next, draw on a region of the screen to be used for the hyperlink.

Figure 45

Next, you will select the page to be hyperlinked and save it. Now, launch the web browser and click on the hot spot to test it. For this example the rectangular hotspot tool was used. However, the circle tools works the same way.

The hotspots will be lost if you replace the picture that they are linked to.

Publishing the

Project Website

**WEB   SERVER   OR
SHARE DRIVE NEEDED**

In this chapter you will learn how to publish your Project Website to a server so that it can be accessed by others.

P ublishing is the term used to describe the process of copying your website files from your local computer to a remote web server. The copying process is not much different from copying files from a CD to your local computer. It could literally be a drag and drop or just a couple of mouse clicks. You will typically publish your entire site once and only publish updates or new files afterwards. You can copy your files to a share drive, but the performance will be slow and access will be limited to the local segment of the network. A web server is simply another computer on the local network or internet that is running web server software. The hardware could be a laptop, desktop or a more robust dedicated server. Web browsers send requests for files to the web servers. The web server software listens for its specific file requests and simply returns the files to the user that requested them. If the file is a web page then it will be displayed in the web browser using HTML formatting. Otherwise, it will open the file in its native application such as MS Word or MS Excel. The most common web server software in use today is Apache, which runs on just about any hardware or operating system. The other most common web server is Microsoft Internet Information Server (IIS), which only runs under Microsoft Windows. Web servers can serve hundreds of files to hundreds of users within a matter of seconds depending onthe file sizes and network speed.

To publish your project website, you will need about **100 megabyte (MB)** of storage space on a web server. As a frame of reference, 100 MB is about 1/6 of a CD or $1/10^{th}$ of a Gigabyte. This is a fairly trivial amount of storage for most web servers today, which store hundreds of Gigabytes. Depending on the project you may need more or less server space.

Intranet Web Servers

If you are working within a company, its corporate network is considered an Intranet. This means that only users within the company have access to the web server. It is typically protected by a security firewall, which is a computer that blocks access from outsiders. Usually, company employees around the world would have access.

Server Environments - Web servers usually fall into four categories:

Development Servers – Development servers are used by the software programmers to store early versions of their applications once they are ready to share them with others. They are typically not very fast servers and may go down for maintenance often as content is continually being added and deleted. Members of the project team typically have access to these servers. These servers are typically administered by the developers.

Test Servers – Once the developers are comfortable with their code, they promote it to test servers. Test servers are used by software testing teams to determine if the software is meeting requirements and specifications. Often, the defects are found and the code is recycled back to the developers. Often end users perform User Acceptance Testing at this level. Test Servers may also be accessible by members of the project team. These servers are typically administered by the developers as well.

Staging Servers – Once the users and testers are satisfied with the code, they authorize it to be promoted to Staging, which is usually an exact replica of the final Production environment. These servers are typically administered by Web Administrators who are also often responsible for security.

Production Servers – If the code runs smoothly in staging it is then promoted to Production where it is accessible by end users. The Production web servers are typically very fast and very robust with backup systems to prevent service interruptions.

Production servers are almost always administered by web administrators who are not a part of the development group. Developers are never allowed access to Production servers. Most don't want the liability.

Going Live on the Intranet – Typically, the easiest intranet server to gain access to is the development webserver. Organizations typically have several of these. Its better to get one that is in the server room if it's a large organization, so it will be backed up regularly. Otherwise, a desktop PC under someone's desk may suffice in a pinch. As long the server is connected to the network and is running web server software, it can "serve" your pages. To store your PM Website on a corporate intranet you will need to have administrator rights on the web server or ask a developer that has administrator rights to provide you with a folder and space for your website. If you have your website on a thumb drive or CD, they can usually copy them to the server in a matter of minutes and give you a URL. Your website will then be **Live** on the intranet.

Internet Web Servers

If you are going to share your web content with people outside of a corporate network i.e. the internet community, then you will need an Internet Web Server. Internet web servers come in a large variety but can roughly be categorized as Windows or Unix platforms. You will also need a web address otherwise known as a Domain Name. It's possible to build your own internet web server from your home or office but the topic is beyond the scope of this book.

Many companies offer web hosting services and most also provide the domain registration. The basic steps are as follows:

1. **Check for Domain Name availability** - Browse to www.betterwhois.com or a similar site to check availability.

2. **Find a hosting service** - This may include free space provided by your cable company or a web hosting company found on the internet. They usually charge about $10 per month. The more space and traffic bandwidth the better. Also, packages that offer web statistics are better. I would shy away from companies that are too large that offer no support. You will know there is no support if you can't find their telephone number! You can purchase the hosting service on-line in a matter of minutes along with the Domain name.

3. **MS Front Page Extensions** - If the site is a Unix or Linux site you will need to have them turn on MS Front Page Extensions. The Servers will work just like a Windows server with the extensions. Some services will give you a control panel where you can simply select option to add MS Front page extensions. You will also need to pick a username and password to access the server through a control panel. Pick a good password with a combination of characters and write it down.

4. **Website Propagation** - After you purchase the domain name and hosting service it usually takes about 24 – 48 hours for the domain name to become fully associated with the server. This is because the routers around the world have to receive your new address in their tables. After propagation, you website will be accessible by users everywhere. But you will need to load your pages remotely, which is the topic of the next section.

Remote Publishing to Web Servers

In most situations, your hosting service will be in another geographic location. Therefore, you will not be able to physically load your website from a CD onto the Web server. Therefore you will need to access the server over the local or wide area network and load your pages remotely. There are several methods that may be used to load your pages remotely:

WARNING

You should try not to use FTP to transfer files as it can damage the FrontPage extensions.

As mentioned above, you will need to have MS FrontPage extensions installed if you are using an UNIX or LINUX server, which is fairly common. Again, publishing simply means you that you will upload your website files to the server. Once this is done, your pages will be viewable from the web.

Publishing MS Front Page

The procedure varies depending on the hosting service, but basically follows this pattern:

1. Launch Microsoft FrontPage

2. Select **File | Publish Site**

3. If this is the first time you publish to the server, select **More Webs** and enter the **Domain Name** you want to publish your Project Website to. (www.yourdomain.com)

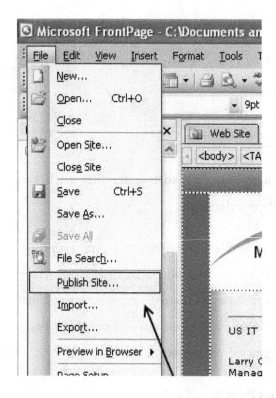

Figure 46

Note: If you have published to the server before, your "Destination Web Server" (www.yourdomain.com) will appear in the Publish window.

IMPORTANT: Use yourdomain.com as the Destination Web Server to publish to the server. Leave the "Destination Web Name" blank.

Figure 47

4. You will be asked for your USERNAME and PASSWORD. This is your domain's User ID and your FrontPage Password. If you're not sure what it is or if you aren't allowed past this point, you'll need to contact your hosting service for a new FrontPage password. You will also need to enter your domain name in the appropriate field.

5. You will then be connected to the server and are ready to publish your Project Website.

Left Window

Once you connect to the remote server you will see two windows. The window on the left is your local computer. This should be pointing to the folder on your local computer that stores your Project website. If this is not the case, use **File | Open Site** to open the website folder.

Right Window:

The window on the right will contain the folders and files contained within your home directory. This is your space on the remote server. This is where you will place your website. You may see folders with names such as www, infobots and access-log.

6. You are now ready to select the Publish button and publish your website to the www directory on the remote server.

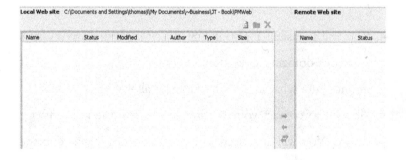

Figure 48

Going Live on the Internet

Select **Publish Website.** You will begin to see the progression of the Project Website files as they are copied to the remote server. Once the copy is complete, select **View your Remote Website.** You will see your Project Website and so will the rest of the world.

Site Maintenance

Once your Project Website is published and online, you will need to access it to make updates and changes. Be sure that you are connected to the internet before attempting to open your web on the remote server.

1. Open FrontPage and choose **File | Open Site** or **File | Recent Sites**

Typically, you will open your site on your PC although its possible to open the version on the remote server as well.

3. Highlight the appropriate web and select **OK.**

4. Enter your Username and Password if required. Usually, the first time during the session its required, but not needed after that unless you close the session.

5. Now that the site is open, you can open the files that want to modify and make changes as necessary. When you are ready to publish the files you can simply save them using **File | Save** and then **File | Publish Web**.

Troubleshooting

The following are common error messages and solutions encountered with using FrontPage

Root Web Busy

FTP or SSH to your site and remove the "**service.lck**" file in /www/_vti_pvt. This usually happens when a FrontPage session is interrupted before completion.

Server times out when publishing large sites.

This difficulty arises when the uploading link times out in the process of copying the web to our server. The only suggestion Microsoft has offered so far is to break the main web into a group of sub webs on your PC, then upload these individually.

Front Page Extensions not Installed

We often see this error being reported even when the extensions have been installed. If you get this error, contact the hosting service support and they will make sure the extensions are installed and repair them if necessary.

NOTE: The extensions are easily corrupted. Please use only FrontPage to update your web site on the server. Never use FTP unless it's the last resort.

I published but my web's not there!

This will happen when the **"Destination Web Name"** is filled in when publishing to the remote server. This box should be left blank. If you put any other name in this box it will create a subdirectory off of your root web and copy all of your files into it. Your site will exist under a subdirectory instead of at the top level /www where it should be.

My counter, bbs, guestbook, etc isn't working.

These problems are generally due to incorrect permissions on the directory, file(s) or cgi script(s) that are associated with them. You will have to contact the hosting service to insure that the permissions are set properly. Don't change the permissions of your files or directories unless you have been instructed by the hosting service support to do so.

The call to a cgi script using the Secure Server must not be within a webbot. Use a normal cgi call in your html script for Secure Server calls.

My search bot doesn't return any results.

The /www directory must be world readable AND you need to recalculate links BEFORE publishing (or after editing directly on the server). If it still doesn't work: FTP to the server and go to the /www/_vti_txt/default.wti directory. Delete any files that begin with "ALL.". Don't delete any other files. Then using Windows Explorer, do the same thing on your PC. Recalculate links, test locally with your browser and publish.

MS Front Page starts the Web Publishing Wizard when I try to publish.

Cancel the operation and contact support to have the MS Front Page extensions installed/repaired.

Why is my page renamed on the server when I publish?

The "Default Document" of your web is automatically renamed by the server to what is required by the configuration of the server. For example, if you've named the main page "index.html", it may be renamed "default.html". Just check the links to your main page to make sure they refer to it the same way.

I have tried everything and still can not publish my site, I am using a Window Server.

If you have permissions on the server, Select Start | Run and enter the "MSTSC" command to terminal serve into the server. You will be prompted for credentials. The remote servers screen will appear on your computer and you can drag and drop the files into the web server directory. If you don't have permissions see the server administrator.

I have tried everything and still can not publish my site, I am using a Linux or Unix Server.

If you have permission to access the server, you will need to acquire an FTP program such as Cute FTP or WSFTP. Some organizations will have their own Remote Administrator tools for their staff's use. If you don't have permissions see the server administrator.

PM Website Tools

Cute FTP® - Optional
Paint.Net® - Recommended
MS Front Page ® - Required (2003
        recommended)
MS Paint ® - Optional
MS Project® - Recommended
MS Word® - Required
MS Notepad® - Required
WS FTP® - Optional
WBS PRO® - Optional

Definitions

These words are used often in this book, so you may want to learn them early.

Domain Name – The name that is purchased to represent web site such as www.PMWebsiteBook.com. It is the part of the name that comes after the www. The name points to the actual server where the web pages are stored. The domain name can be used interchangeably with the IP address of the server, which his much harder to remember. A Domain Name Service is used to automatically translate the domain name into the ip address. Typically, domain names are purchased for about $25 US per year. If a Domain Name expires you can still access the files using the server IP address.

e-Business – The process of utilizing web technologies to perform conventional business practices to drive higher level performance, efficiency and profits.

e- Commerce – The process of buying and selling on the internet.

Extranet – A limited part of an intranet that is used by outside customers or suppliers. See intranet

Firewall – A hardware or software device that controls access to the network. It can block or allow specific protocols, users, applications, etc.

GIF - Graphics Interchange Format – GIFs are very common photo formats used on the web. They are typically small and render very quickly. The are best used when they do not contain a lot of colors. GIFs support animation and do not lose resolution.

HTML – Hyper Text Markup Language – The predominant format used on the internet to modify the display of text on the computer screen.

Hyperlink – A function that allows a user to connect to other web pages by simply mouse clicking on text, pictures, or other web objects within a page.

Internet – A large global computer network composed of many smaller networks that is accessible by the general public and most any organization

Intranet – A network that is internal to an organization. It can not be accessed by the public.

JPEG – Also, JPG – Joint Picture Experts Group – JPG files are designed to be compressed by losing some amount of resolution. This allows them to display much quicker on the web.

LAN - Local Area Network – A LAN is group of computers that are connected together typically in a single building. These are usually connected through wires that run to a central switch. The most common protocol used to communicate between computers is Ethernet.

Pixel - The unit of measurement on the web. One pixel is approximately the size of a period (.) in 12-point Arial font.

PNG - Portable Network Graphics – PNG photos compress more than GIF files and do not lose resolution. They use an open standard and do not have the copyright issues associated with GIFs.

Portfolio Management – Portfolio Management is the process of managing a group of projects through their lifecycle. This may include maintenance, which is not a part of project management.

Program Management – Management of a group of similar projects.

Project Management Office (PMO) – The formal branch of an organization that is responsible for providing project guidance, standards and governance.

Project Management Professional (PMP) – A person that has met the education/experience requirements, has successfully passed the PM examination and is certified by the Project Management Institute as a project manager.

Project – A temporary endeavor to create a unique product or service with a defined beginning and end.

Project Management – The process of overseeing a project through its phases including initiating, planning, executing, controlling and closing.

Project Manager – The individual in charge of and responsible for completing the project on time, within budgeting and meeting the requirements for which it was undertaken.

Publishing – In web development, this is the process of transferring content from a development workstation to a production server to make it available to users.

Rendering – For photos, rendering is the process of decompressing an image and displaying it on the screen.

Router – A hardware device that forwards packets of data across the wide area network. Then internet is composed of a series of interconnected routers, which for the world wide web.

Resolution – The concentration of pixels that form an image. The more pixels the higher the resolution, the less pixels the lower the resolution. If an image is 1,000 pixels wide by 1,000 pixels long it is 1,000,000 pixels or 1 mega pixel.

Switch – A hardware device that connects computers within a building. Switches typically run at 100Megabit to 1,000 Megabit. If the data has to go beyond the building then it typically goes out through a router.

URL (Universal Resource Locator) - The address of a web site. This is what is after the "http://" on the location bar on your browser.

WLAN – A wireless LAN that typically runs at either 11Mb or 54Mb.

Website – A page or set of pages that describe content that is stored on local and remote server. The designer determines which content to include or not include.

Wide Area Network – The set of interconnected but geographically separated routers that make up the network, such as the internet.

References

Fleming, Quinten W. and Koppelman, Joel (2000) Earned Value Project Management, 2nd ed., Project Management Institute. ISBN 1-880410-27-3

Project Management Institute (2003). A Guide To The Project Management Body Of Knowledge, 3rd ed., Project Management Institute. ISBN 1-930699-45-X.

Kerzner, Harold (2003). Project Management: A Systems Approach to Planning, Scheduling, and Controlling, 8th Ed., Wiley. ISBN 0-471-22577-0.

Flyvbjerg, Bent, (2006). "From Nobel Prize to Project Management: Getting Risks Right." Project Management Journal, vol. 37, no. 3, pp. 5-15..

Berkun, Scott (2005). Art of Project Management. Cambridge, MA: O'Reilly Media. ISBN 0-596-00786-8.

Comninos D &, Frigenti E (2002). The Practice of Project Management - a guide to the business-focused approach. Kogan Page. ISBN 0-7494-3694-8

Heerkens, Gary (2001). Project Management (The Briefcase Book Series). McGraw-Hill. ISBN 0-07-137952-5.

Chamoun, Yamal (2006). Professional Project Management, THE GUIDE, 1st.Edition, Monterrey, NL MEXICO: McGraw Hill. ISBN 970-10-5922-0.

Lewis, James (2002). Fundamentals of Project Management, 2nd ed., American Management Association. ISBN 0-8144-7132-3.

Meredith, Jack R. and Mantel, Samuel J. (2002). Project Management : A Managerial Approach, 5th ed., Wiley. ISBN 0-471-07323-7.

Stellman, Andrew and Greene, Jennifer (2005). Applied Software Project Management. Cambridge, MA: O'Reilly Media. ISBN 0-596-00948-8.

Thayer, Richard H. and Yourdon, Edward (2000). Software Engineering Project Management, 2nd Ed., Wiley-IEEE Computer Society Press. ISBN 0-8186-8000-8.

Index

www.ingramcontent.com/pod-product-compliance
Lightning Source LLC
Chambersburg PA
CBHW071225050326
40689CB00011B/2465